Early Loggers and the Sawmill

Peter Adams

The Early Settler Life Series

 Toronto New York

Crabtree Publishing Company

To my mother

Special thanks to *Bobbie Kalman, Lori Pattenden, Nancy Cook, Tom Nagy, Ken McPherson, Wally D. Bonner, Sarah Peters, Peter Logan, Andrea Crabtree, Stephanie Williams, Trish Holman, Barbara Snyder and Bill Patterson.*

Copyright © 1981, 1989, 1992 Crabtree Publishing Company

Cataloging in Publication Data

Adams, Peter.
  Early Loggers and the Sawmill

(Early settler life series)
Includes index.
ISBN   0–86505–005–8 hardcover
ISBN   0–86505–006–6 softcover

1. Lumbering – History. 2. Sawmills – History.
3. Logging – History. I. Title. II. Series.

SD 538. A 32   634. 9'82'097   C 81–094758–7
LC 93-6245

350 Fifth Ave, Suite 3308
New York, NY 10118

R.R. #4
360 York Road
Niagara-on-the-Lake, ON
Canada L0S 1J0

73 Lime Walk
Headington, Oxford 0X3 7AD
United Kingdom

Contents

While his wife and children watch from their log cabin, an early settler, helped by his neighbor, cuts down trees to make his second field. The grain in his first field is doing

The early settler and the forest

Every pioneer was a logger and a lumberman. A logger cuts down trees, while a lumberman makes money by selling the cut trees to someone who needs the wood. The early settler did both.

When early settlers came to the section of land they were going to farm, they did not find clear fields ready to plough. Except on the prairies, they usually found a forest. They had to cut the

forest down before they could plant their seeds and grow grain and vegetables for their family.

Land in return for work

Early settlers were often given a section of land in return for clearing it. The land was their payment for the hard work of cutting down the trees and digging out the huge roots.

well. His family and farm animals will have bread and grain to eat during the winter.

The settler had to work quickly. Trees had to be cut down and crops grown before the supplies ran out. The settler family might go hungry. They would then have to return to a town to find work. The dream of being a farmer would have to wait.

The family only had a *lean-to* to live in at first. A lean-to was a temporary shelter made of branches or logs attached to a supporting pole in the ground and sloping in one direction. The settlers had to quickly build a better shelter for themselves.

The first home consisted of four corner posts stuck into the earth. The walls were made by standing saplings (young trees) side by side. It was easy for the settler to cut down the thin saplings. The roof was made by laying saplings side by side with branches on top. The leaves on the branches kept out the rain. The family could make this shelter in a short time. Then they could quickly start clearing the forest for farming.

In this old drawing his wife prepares food for the farm animals in front of their log cabin, while a farmer starts clearing a second field. The wheat from his first harvest is stacked behind their cabin. He still has to pull the roots out of his first field.

Clearing the land

There were three ways settlers could clear the trees from their land. First, they could hold a logging *bee*. Bees were held for all sorts of large settler jobs such as house-building, barn-raising, quilting blankets, and harvesting. In a bee all the settlers in one area joined together to help a neighbor get a big job done quickly.

The logging bee

In a logging bee the neighbors brought their axes and their oxen. They chopped the trees down. Their oxen pulled out the roots. In return for their help the settler would give the neighbors food and drink, and, of course, help *them* when they needed it.

Though the work was done quickly, there were problems with logging-bees. They could be expensive if there were a great many neighbors to feed. Also, it was hard work preparing three meals a day for the workers. Sometimes the neighbors drank too much alcohol. They would quarrel and fight or else lie about and sleep. Sometimes very little work was done.

But if everyone worked hard a bee could allow a new settler to plough his fields and sow his seeds in time for a good fall harvest. The family would have enough food to last through the hard months of their first winter.

Do it yourself

Settlers could chop the large trees down by themselves and then set fire to the thick underbrush. The underbrush is all the bushes and young trees that grow between the larger trees. The fire was dangerous. It could grow out of control. If the wind shifted, the fire could kill the settler's family before they could escape.

Axes for rent

Settlers could hire special Contract Choppers to clear their land. The settlers would feed the Contract Choppers and give them a bed while they chopped the trees. When the Contract Choppers were finished, the settlers would pay them for their work. Only the richer settlers ha enough money to pay Contract Choppers.

Leaning on their axes, two Contract Choppers pause while turning a forest into a farmer's field.

This machine pulled roots out of the ground. A chain was attached to the root and to a screw above it. Oxen walked the machine around in a circle. This turned the screw upwards, pulling out the root.

In this old photograph a new settler has time to fish. He has planted his second summer's crops. He has finished his log cabin. But he must take the stumps out of his field.

The log cabin

After the settlers had cleared enough land for their first crop and after the seed was planted, they had time to build their first house, a log cabin.

A log cabin was usually square with sides about six metres long. Its walls were usually three metres high. Logs were placed one on top of the other. A half circle was cut out of the bottom of each log so that it would fit snugly around the top of the log below. Gaps between the logs were filled with a mixture of mud, clay and sand. It hardened like cement and kept the rain and the wind out.

The roof was made with saplings or small trees. Large slabs of bark were laid on top of the saplings. The rain ran off the roof along the troughs of bark.

The settler had to cut windows and doors out of the large logs with a hand saw. This was such hard work that many log cabins had only a door and no windows. It was too costly and difficult to obtain glass. Paper was dipped in oil to make a transparent substitute.

The floor was often just packed down mud. Sometimes bark was laid on the mud to control the dirt. Before a fireplace could be built on one side of the cabin, the only fireplace was a heap of stones in the middle of the cabin. The smoke went out a hole in the roof.

In this old photograph a family has just completed their log cabin. They have not yet filled the spaces between the logs with moss or clay to keep out the wind and rain. They have added one extra log on the top of the front wall. This has slanted the roof so the rain will run off toward the back of the house. The roof is made of half logs that have been hollowed out. One log is placed front up. The next log is back up. The rain runs into the hollow and off the house. The log cabin on page 6 has this type of roof.

Two early settlers whipsaw a log into thin planks. One person stands above the log. Another person stands beneath it. Before a sawmill was built in their area, whipsawing was the only way settlers could cut a log into planks. Whipsawing was hard, slow work.

How the early settler worked with wood

Early settlers constantly needed wood. They needed it for houses, barns, furniture and boxes. Everything they used seemed to be made out of wood. Even the yoke that held the settler's oxen together was made from wood.

Before there was a sawmill in their area, the settlers had to get their wood from the forest around them. After they cut the trees down, the settlers had to slowly cut them into smaller pieces of wood that could be used to make yokes or boxes.

The settlers did not have a saw powered by water. They only had muscle power. If they wanted to turn a round tree into straight, thin planks, they had to use a whipsaw. One man stood on top of the log while another man sawed from underneath. It would take hours to whipsaw a few planks.

Settlers needed wood of different lengths and widths. They found it difficult to obtain all the wood they needed by using hand saws to cut it. A sawmill was needed.

Because whipsawing a log into planks took so long, often early settlers just squared the log before building their houses. They used a broadax.

Settlers show their woodworking tools; (l. to r.) a chisel, a mallet, a pick, an auger for drilling holes and an adze for scooping out wood. Photo taken in 1864.

A farm hand slowly smooths a piece of wood. Later the sawmill will give him finished wood he can use right away.

A farmer uses a club to knock roof shingles off a block of wood. Later a sawmill will cut shingles more easily.

The plank house

After a sawmill was built in an area, settlers there could build better homes than their log cabins. They could build homes made with planks cut at the sawmill.

To build a plank house the settler first put up the wooden frame. Then the planks were nailed to the frame. The planks fit together very tightly. Sometimes the planks had a small tongue on one edge so that they overlapped each other. The wind and the rain could not get between the planks. There were no gaps between the planks that needed to be filled with mud.

With planks from the sawmill, settlers could make other improvements to their houses. They could make smooth wooden floors. They could put a second floor on their houses because the frame of the house could support the lightweight planks. Settlers could also easily section off their houses into rooms with the boards from the sawmill.

With planks or boards it was easier for the settler to have large windows in his house. It was also easier for the settlers to build many out-buildings or dependencies for their farms, such as a carriage shed, a barn for the grain and the cows, a stable for the horses, a pig pen, a chicken coop and an ash house for smoking meat.

The settlers have farmed in this area for a number of years. Most of the trees have been cut down, and the stumps pulled out. The settlers have large fields. They have built a bridge over the river. They have good roads over which they can easily visit their neighbors. The settlers also have a sawmill in the area. It is the building right behind the bridge. On the ground beside the sawmill are piles of planks and boards. These

Planks were cut from logs in the sawmill. The farmers have used the planks to build barns, tool sheds, chicken coops and pig pens, as well as their homes. Planks and squared logs from the sawmill also were used to make the bridge. The farmers' fences are also made from wood cut at the sawmill.

The settler who built the sawmill dammed up the river to create a pond behind the saw-mill. You can see logs floating in the pond. He then allowed some of the water from the pond to rush under his sawmill. This turned the saw that cut the logs into planks.

Our world is a plastic one. The early settler world was a wooden one. Flour is being shipped in wooden barrels on wooden barges. Inspectors test the flour by boring holes. The boy on the right plugs up the hole. Poor women wait to scoop up any spilled flour.

A world of wood

This sawyer cuts wood into small pieces at a sawmill so that craftspeople can make boxes and barrels with it.

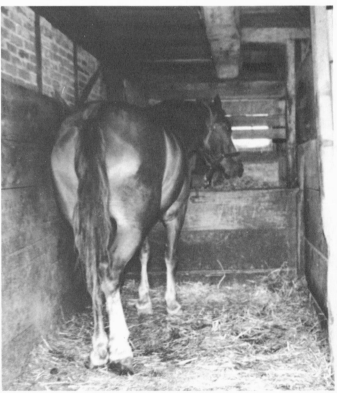

Wooden planks are used by a farmer to build a stall in his stable.

Andrea makes yarn with her family's wooden spinning wheel.

Wainwrights used wood to make wagons, as well as some iron to hold it all together.

Farmers wash sheep on a wooden bridge. A wooden fence corrals the frightened sheep. What else is made from wood?

A wooden hut keeps a well sheltered. Wooden shingles cover the roof. Wooden planks cover the house.

The cabinetmaker made all sorts of cabinets; cabinets that were cupboards as well as cabinets for grandfather clocks and wall clocks. The cabinetmaker also made chairs, tables and four-poster beds. The cabinetmaker needed wood from the sawmill for the furniture. A plank is waiting in the back of the shop to be made into a table top.

Village craftspeople needed the sawmill

The early settler village had many craftspeople who needed wood; the wheelwright, the gunsmith, the cabinetmaker, the cooper, the musical instrument maker. Pictures of these craftspeople are on these pages.

There were other craftspeople who needed wood, such as the wainwright who made the wagons, sleighs and carriages. The harness maker also needed wood to make saddle seats and neck yokes for horses and oxen. The joiner was the carpenter who finished off the interior of homes, making stairs and paneling the rooms with

wood. The joiner also needed wood from the sawmill.

These craftspeople did not have the time to cut down trees and then whipsaw planks. They relied on the sawmill giving them wood of different lengths and widths that they could use in their businesses.

The sawmill made the community a more pleasant place in which to live. It helped many people. It helped the craftspeople and it helped the settlers who used the craftspeoples' creations.

The gunsmith made flintlock guns. The gunsmith needed wood from the sawmill to carve the stock of the gun.

The wheelwright made wheels for wagons and carriages. Curved wood for a wheel rim is under the bench.

Musical instrument makers needed wood. The harpsichord (an early piano) and the violin are both made of wood.

Coopers made barrels. Coopers needed wood for the sides and tops and bottoms of their barrels.

The early sawmill

When a new community began to grow, its people needed wood to build their houses. Craftspeople required wood to make all the furniture, carriages, household articles and farming tools that people needed to live from day to day. A person would use his money to build a sawmill to give everyone the wood they needed. The person who built the sawmill was called the miller or the sawyer. A sawyer is a person who saws wood for a living.

A person who spends his money to start a business is called an *entrepreneur*. The person who built the sawmill was an entrepreneur. Often the person who built the sawmill made a lot of money selling planks to the other people in the community. The sawyer would become an important person in the community. The sawyer might also build a grist mill on the river near the sawmill. Then he would also grind the farmer's grain and make more money.

While the sawyer is cutting the logs into boards, two men with poles are pushing another log up into the sawmill. The cut planks are piled at the foot of the hill ready for a buyer to take them.

18

The miller has built his sawmill beside a fast-moving river. The rushing water hits a wheel under the sawmill. The water turns the wheel around causing the saw to go up and down and cut the logs. A blockhouse used by soldiers as a fort stands on the hill.

19

Building a sawmill in 1833

These four pictures show a sawmill being built in 1833. The first step in building a sawmill was the making of the millpond. To make the deep pond the river had to be dammed up. The men are building the dam with logs. The logs will hold the water back. The river will widen and deepen into a small lake or pond behind the dam.

The dam is complete. The water is falling over the wall or dam making a small waterfall. The height of the river behind the waterfall has been raised about six feet. This has widened and deepened the river into a pond. The sawmill will be built on this side of the three upright logs. The water rushing between the logs will turn a wheel under the sawmill. When the wheel turns it will cause the saw to go up and down and cut the logs.

These men are cutting down trees. The logs are being used to build the sawmill. The frame of the sawmill can be seen on the river. It is being built below the milldam. The men are cutting trees beside the pond above the milldam. The man in the center is holding a tripod. He is a land surveyor. He is measuring the land to decide where to put the roads in the new town that will grow up beside the sawmill.

The finished sawmill is hard at work cutting boards. Logs float in the millpond waiting for the men to haul them up the ramp to the saw. Cut planks spill out of the sawmill. They will be piled. You can see the three upright logs in front of the sawmill where the water from the pond rushes down below the sawmill. The sawyer can stop this water from turning the waterwheel below the saw. When the wheel stops, the saw stops.

In this old photograph a sawyer stands proudly beside his sawmill. He built it himself. He spent all the money he had to build the mill. Now he makes enough money selling lumber (boards) to build a house for his family and to buy food and clothes for them. The sawyer built his mill beside a little creek leading into the ocean. To make the water from the creek rush more strongly against his waterwheel, he dammed up the creek. The dam is just the other side of the two rowboats. When the sawyer let the water from the pond rush against the slats of his waterwheel, the waterwheel turned. This turned the saw which cut the wood.

Water power

Sawmills were built so that water did all the work. Sawmills were built beside rivers. The force of the rushing water was used to make the saw go. If the river was not a fast one, the sawmill owner often dammed up the river to make a large pond. When he opened the dam, the water flowed fast enough to turn the waterwheel. The turning waterwheel turned a series of shafts inside the sawmill. These turning shafts caused the saw to go either up and down as in a muley saw or around as in a circular of rotary saw.

Here is another sawmill beside a dammed-up river. The men are pushing logs from a log boom in the millpond to the sawmill. Rushing water from the millpond turns a waterwheel inside the mill.

This sawyer is running a muley saw, the first type of saw in sawmills. The muley saw only moved up and down. It cut logs slowly because it only cut on the down strokes.

The muley saw

The sawyer is standing on the carriage that pulls the log toward the muley saw.

The millrace or water channel leads water from the pond to the waterwheel.

Pike men use their poles to herd logs toward the sawmill. A chain with hooks pulled the logs up the steep ramp into the sawmill. The men at the top of the ramp moved the logs to the carriage that carried the logs to the saw.

A place of action

A sawmill was an active, noisy place. Everyone had a job to do. If a job was not done correctly, a person could be crushed by a log or have a hand cut off by the saw.

Pike men poled logs toward the mill ramp. Persons at the top of the ramp directed the logs toward the saw carriage.

Other persons lifted the heavy logs onto the saw carriage. Then other sawyers on the carriage pulled levers that moved the carriage toward the whirring saw. With a roar the saw ripped into the wood. Sawdust flew through the air, choking the sawyers on the saw carriage. The roar of the saw hurt their ears.

As planks were cut from the log and fell to the ground, off-loaders rushed forward to carry the boards to sorting tables. Boards of equal length were piled together in the yard behind the mill.

The upright muley saw was slow because it only cut on the downward stroke. To cut the log more quickly a saw was needed whose teeth continually cut into the logs. The circular saw was invented. As the circular saw whirred around, its teeth were always biting into the wood. The sawyer could cut many more boards each day.

This 1872 photograph shows how water flowing under the mill carries logs toward the saw-mill's three ramps. You can see the chains on the ramps that catch the bark of the log, pulling the log up the ramp.

This picture shows the other side of the sawmill at the top of the page on the same day in 1872. The saws have cut the logs into boards. Mill hands are loading the lumber on the company's carts to be delivered to builders and craftspeople throughout the city.

In picture 1, mill hands take a well-earned rest on half-cut logs. 2) A man with a peavy moves forward to wrestle a huge log onto the saw carriage. 3) The sawyers move the carriage and the log against the circular rotary saw, which replaced the muley saw. 4) The mill hands walk home past the huge incinerator or furnace that was used to burn up the leftover sawdust and small pieces of wood. It had a screen on top so large sparks couldn't escape and set fire to the sawmill. 5) This is the man who kept the sawmill busy. He is the chopper working in the wilderness, miles away from any village. His axe started a tree's journey from a tall forest monarch to a pile of boards.

You are looking toward the sawmill doors through which the logs are brought from the millpond. You can see three logs on their carriages. They are moving toward band saws which had four or more vibrating upright saws that sliced a log into several boards at once. The band saw became popular after 1885.

Workers cut firewood for kitchen stoves and living room fireplaces in the mill yard.

In this old photograph, a worker in a finishing mill sands the wood on a cupboard door so that it becomes very smooth. It will look beautiful when stained.

Making fine, smooth wood in the finishing mill

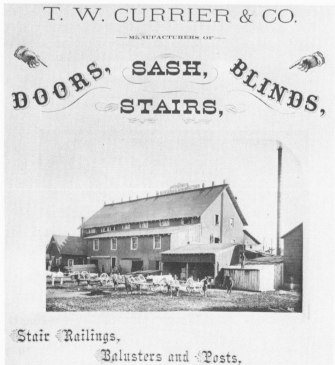

The plank that was cut by the saw in the sawmill was often very rough. The cabinet maker or the joiner would have to spend a lot of time sanding the wood before they could use it.

Also some craftsmen needed wood that was bent or curved. Both the wheelwright and the wainwright needed curved wood.

To give the craftspeople the finished wood they needed, the sawmill owner often started a finishing mill beside the sawmill.

Before long the sawmill owner began to compete with the craftspeople. He began to make doors and stair railings. He sold them directly to the house builders.

◄ *The man in the top picture worked in the finishing mill shown in this 1875 advertisement.*

These men have placed long pieces of wood in the oven. Boiling water in the oven steamed the wood. After an hour in the oven, the hot, wet wood was very easy to bend.

Men bend the wood after taking it from the oven. They are bending the wood into shapes that are used in making horse carriages.

The mill owner is sitting on the pile of boards. He is the third person from the right in the front row. Sitting around him are sawyers and mill hands he has hired. They all work a long day. They work from sunrise to sunset to cut all the boards the town needs.

The sawmill was a family affair

A sawmill was usually a family business. The father would build the mill and his sons would work in it. Usually the wife and daughters did not work in the mill. They stayed at home. They prepared the meals and cleaned the clothes and the rooms. If there were small family-owned sawmills today, the girls as well as the boys would run the saw and attach the logs to the carriage and stack the boards in the yard.

When the father died or was too old to run the mill, his sons carried on. Their sons in turn would run the mill when they died or became too old to work. If the son was too young to run the mill when his father died, the mother would often take over the mill.

In larger mills extra men had to be hired. They were called sawyers. They often lived in the sawmill owner's house as boarders. They ate with the family. They received money as well as food to eat and a room in which to sleep.

Often the sawyer received wheat or butter or a chicken from the miller instead of money. This was necessary because the miller had received them instead of money from the farmers who were his customers. He passed the meat and grain along to his sawyers.

The sawyers traded these products at the general store for things they needed, such as tobacco, pipes, long winter underwear and heavy boots.

When the water froze around the water-wheel in the winter, the wheel could not turn to power the saw. Therefore, in the summer the mill had to run day and night to cut enough lumber for the community to use all year round.

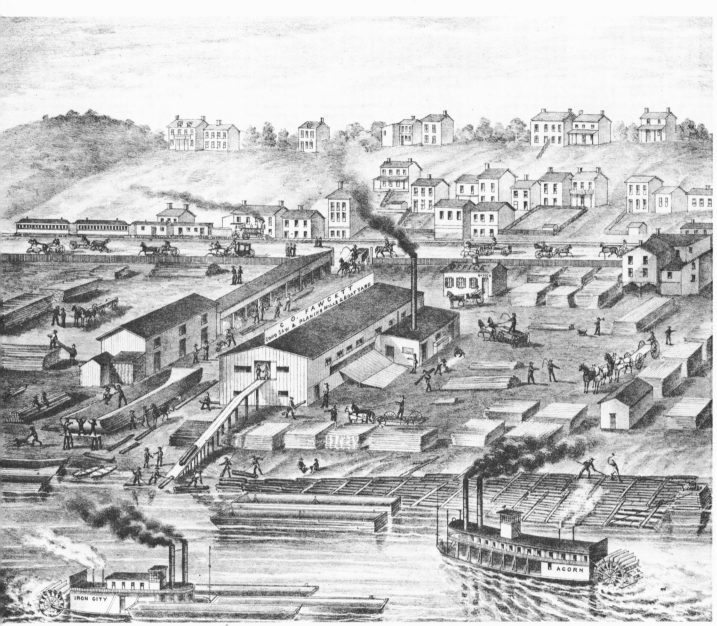

Mr. Fawcett used the boards cut in the sawmill to build boats. A barge is being built beside the sawmill. It is like the barges being pushed by the paddlewheeler, Iron City. The logs to be cut in the sawmill are kept beside the shore in a large boom. The boom is broken up log by log. The logs are sent up the ramp to the saw. Mr. Fawcett advertises that his mill is a sawmill and a planing mill. The sawmill cut rough planks for use in building houses or boats. The planing mill smoothed or planed the boards for craftspeople such as the cabinetmaker to use.

Dangerous for children

The sawmill was a dangerous place for children to play as accidents in the mill were common. Most people working in the mill were missing one or more fingers.

However, the miller's children did have chores to do. Sometimes the older children clamped the logs onto the carriage that carried them into the saw.

The children were often responsible for oiling the metal moving parts in the mill to keep them working smoothly and to prevent them from rusting.

The children also took turns sweeping the sawdust away from the working area. Sometimes the sawdust was burnt. Sometimes it was sold as insulating material. It was poured between the inner and outer wall of a house to keep the cold out in the winter and the heat out in the summer.

In this old 1870 photograph an addition is being built onto the sawmill. The mill owner is busily cutting down all the trees around the mill. There is a huge pile of logs beside the millpond. When all the trees are cut down, the miller will have to pay loggers to go deep into the woods to cut down more trees for him.

Loggers are needed

Wood from far away

When a sawmill was first built, the logs it sawed came from the surrounding land. Farmers brought in trees they had cut down when they cleared their land. The millers often owned some land nearby from which they cut their trees. When there were no big trees left in the area of the sawmill, the miller hired loggers to go far into the bush, cut down the trees and float them down the rivers to the sawmill.

A contract for wood

In the autumn the miller would make a contract with the loggers. He would promise to pay them a certain amount of money for each log they delivered to his mill in the spring. In the autumn the miller would pay for the food, horses and tools that the loggers needed to live in the woods all winter and cut down the trees. In the spring, after the logs had been delivered, the miller deducted the cost of the food, horses and tools from the money he owed for the logs.

A logger's heart must have leaped when he saw these white pines in 1865.

A cruiser has climbed a tree to look at the types of trees growing in the forest.

Cruisers find the perfect trees

Scouts, called cruisers, were sent into the woods in the fall to find the best location in which to set up the lumber camp.

Delivery by river

The camp had to be near a river so the logs could be floated down to the mill.

Trees that make strong houses

The camp had to be near a forest that had a large number of the types of trees the miller wanted. For example, white pine was an excellent hard wood for building and furniture making. It was a large tree and would make many boards.

Farmers meet at the local hotel in the fall. They have harvested their crops. The carts will carry them into the woods to become loggers. The miller who hired them is standing in the foreground. He is telling the farmers how hard they will have to work.

Loggers and supplies head into the bush

Materials for the lumber camp are portaged between lakes on a railroad flat car.

Many loggers were farmers. Since logging operations did not start until the late fall, the farmers had finished harvesting the summer crop. They had the free time to make some extra money during the winter chopping down trees. In the spring the farmers drove the trees down the rivers to the sawmill. They were home in time to plant the next summer's crop. The farmers often took their oxen to the logging camp to pull the logs from the forest to the river.

The farmers missed their families. There was no room in early camps for wives and children. Also, the wives and children had a most important job at home. They had to make sure the pigs, cows, sheep and chickens survived the cold winter.

As soon as they arrived at the spot chosen for their camp, the new loggers had to build a log cabin in which to sleep and cook. The cabin was called a shanty. In this 1870 photograph the shanty is in the background. In the foreground is a log hut for keeping supplies safe from wild animals such as bears, lynx and foxes.

Building the logging camp

When the best part of the forest for logging was found, a shanty for the horses and the loggers was built. In small logging operations the horses were kept in the same building as the loggers. In larger operations there was a separate stable for the horses.

The loggers' shanty had a large fireplace in the center of the building. The fire was used both for cooking and for heating the shanty. There was a large chimney in the roof to let the smoke out. The loggers slept in bunks around the room. As they lay on their backs they could see the moon and stars through the large hole in the roof.

After a hard day of cutting trees and pulling logs out of the forest, loggers relax in the shanty after supper. Some men read newspapers on their bunk beds. Three men play cards. Two men stare into the fire while enjoying a peaceful pipeful of tobacco. One man stirs the tea in the huge pot over the cambuse fire.

Life in the shanty

The loggers slept and ate in the log shanty. In the middle of the shanty was the cambuse fire. The fire both cooked the loggers' food and kept them warm. The logs were burned on top of a mound of sand so the wooden floor wouldn't catch fire. A large hole in the ceiling let the smoke out of the shanty.

Bunks were built around the shanty walls. The loggers lay on their bunks to read and eat or they sat on log benches around the fire. Life in the shanty was often very friendly. The loggers became good friends as they ate and slept side by side in the shanty and worked side by side in the forest.

Their bodies aching, loggers sit in front of their bunks. The straw mattresses or ticks of the upper bunks hang down into the lower bunks. Wet socks hang to dry.

Loggers wait patiently for supper while the cook peels potatoes. With freezing winter air coming down through the hole in the roof, it was best to keep your hat on. Besides cooking the food, the fire also heated the room.

This is the cambuse fire in the middle of the shanty. The cook either boiled food in the pot over the logs or baked food by burying the pot in the hot sand. The cook carries a shovel he uses to bury the pots. Everything was made in a pot; soup, pork 'n beans, pie and tea.

The cook and his best friend, the bean

Food was the most important thing in life to men cutting down trees all day in freezing weather. Often loggers wanted to know the name of the cook before they would join a shanty.

Some cooks with little imagination had a small range of foods: salt pork, barley soup, dried peas and molasses. Better cooks added sugar, tea, butter, jam, and fresh fruit and vegetables.

Cooks had to make their food tasty. They faced fifty hungry men every morning and night. One cook, faced with complaints about his tasteless salt pork, first boiled it in water to get rid of the salt, then cut it into pieces, rolled it in brown sugar and cooked it on a cookie sheet. It may have been bad for the teeth, but it tasted a lot better!

The cook was up at 4 o'clock in the morning preparing breakfast that started at five. One of the breakfasts was oatmeal and prunes - pork and beans on toast - raisin pie - bread, butter and cheese. All meals were washed down with strong, boiling hot tea.

The cook put out pork, bread and cheese so the loggers could make their own lunches. They ate their lunches in the woods. There were two lunches; one at nine o'clock and one at one o'clock.

Supper was the big meal of the day. Here is a typical dinner that was served about seven o'clock. Pea soup - beef, pork and mustard - sugar pie, raisin pie and molasses cookies - bread, butter and cheese - tea and milk.

The loggers were in bed by nine. Loggers often had beans at each meal. Beans didn't spoil. They were easy to carry in sacks into the camp. Chefs boiled them and then baked them with pieces of pork. They were delicious.

Cooks didn't allow talking at meals. If the men couldn't talk they could not complain about the food. And they could not get into arguments that would lead to fights.

The men would take their tin plates and their hunting knives to the cook's pots and spear their own supper. They would then eat the food sitting on their bunks. Each man stuck his knife in the wall over his bunk until the next meal.

In the largest camps, employing over 100 loggers, there was often a separate dining room. These men are talking to each other, but the rule in most camps was "No talking while eating." Cooks just wanted to see the loggers gulping their food down.

The two young men in bowler hats are cookees or cook's helpers.

As the sun sets behind him, the cook trumpets the men in from the woods.

The blacksmith

Blacksmiths kept the horses going in terrible winter weather. They made snowshoes for the horses pulling logs out of deep snow. They made horseshoes with cleats or spikes for horses dragging logs along icy roads. This stopped horses from falling and breaking their legs.

The storekeeper

Larger camps had a store in which the loggers could buy new heavy woolen socks and gloves, heavy woolen mackinaw jackets and blankets. Often loggers had nothing when they arrived. They worked all winter to pay for their clothes and blankets.

You can tell who the foreman is. He is the serious-looking man second from the right. He is teaching some new men the right way to fell a tree. The foreman could do every logger's job better than anyone else in the camp. He was stronger and smarter than anyone else. The foreman's first aid kit is hanging on the axe in the foreground. The foreman was responsible for keeping the loggers working hard every day.

The bull of the woods

Loggers had to be strong, determined men. They worked hard in cold forests. Their work was dangerous. Many loggers were killed by falling trees, crushed under huge sleds or drowned in raging rivers. To survive they had to work as a team.

The leader of the logging team was the foreman. He was the strongest and toughest logger in the camp. The foreman was known as "the bull of the woods".

The foreman knew every job in the lumber camp. He gave orders and every logger instantly obeyed him. Often the loggers would brag about their foreman. One group of loggers said that their foreman was so tough that when he was tired after a day's work he rode a bear

back to the shanty rather than walk. Other loggers boasted that their foreman could kick so high when he was dancing a jig that he left a footprint on the ceiling of their shanty.

The most important job of the foreman was to see that the loggers cut and piled enough logs each day. He had other jobs. He was the doctor who looked after the sick and injured. He would splint a broken arm. He would bandage an axe cut so tightly it healed as if it had been sewn together by a real doctor. He was the storekeeper in charge of supplies. He was the policeman and the judge of the camp. He stopped fights and settled arguments. He was the banker who paid the men their wages at the end of the winter.

The chopper on the right in the top picture is making the undercut. The tree will fall toward his side. The chopper on the left is making the higher back cut. When the two cuts meet the tree will fall. In the middle picture beans and tea are heated in pots for lunch. After chopping since dawn, the men are starving. In the bottom picture two buckers saw the fallen tree into smaller lengths so the horses can drag it out of the bush.

A wet stone for sharpening axes was an important instrument in every shanty. Water was put in the box. As the logger turned the handle, the stone became wet. The water made the stone slide more easily against the blade of the axe, sharpening it.

The choppers

Choppers cut down trees. They kept their axes so sharp they could shave with them. Choppers or fallers had to make the tree fall down exactly where they wanted. They didn't want to hit other choppers. They wanted the log to lie in a place where their horses could pull it easily out of the forest. They made a big undercut on the side toward which they wanted a tree to fall. Then they made a smaller back cut to make the tree fall down.

When the tree was about to topple, the choppers yelled "TIMBER-R-R" to warn the other loggers. Sometimes accidents

happened. One day a tree fell on a logger who was lucky enough to be standing on top of a two metre snowdrift. The falling tree knocked him right to the bottom of the drift. It took a few minutes to dig him out but he survived the blow.

Choppers sometimes cut themselves. They didn't have a doctor to sew them up. Their fellow loggers shoved a plug of chewing tobacco into the hole to stop infection and bound the arm or leg very tightly with a shirt to stop the bleeding. The foreman sewed the chopper up with a needle and thread back at the shanty.

Lumbermen liked some of the logs to be squared. More squared logs could be piled in the hold of a ship for the export trade than round logs. In the early days of logging the tree was squared right where it fell on the forest floor. A string full of chalk was twanged against the side of the tree to show the hewers how much to cut off.

These choppers are preparing the tree for the hewers. The loggers have cut the log so that it is pointed in front. This made it easier to pull it out of the forest. The pointed edge did not get caught as easily against rocks and other trees. It bounded off and kept sliding.

The highly skilled hewers hew or cut to the line made by the chalk. The hewers cut the tree as smooth and straight as the side of a dining room cabinet. The Broadax had a chisel-like blade, perfect for trimming. Squaring a tree was wasteful. It left 25 per cent of the tree on the forest floor. Squaring stopped at the end of the 19th century.

If a tree was not to be exported on a ship, it was not squared. In this 1870 photograph, two choppers fell a tree while three skidders load round logs onto a sled. The horses will pull them out of the forest. The logs will be piled on a skidway. These logs will be cut into boards at a nearby sawmill.

A skidder skids a log over the snow. His sled is called a go-devil. The bark has been taken off the tree to make it slide more easily.

The skidders

The skidders hauled the logs out of the woods to the road. The skidder would attach a chain to the log and also to his horse's harness. The horse, pulling with all its might, would drag out the tree.

Saving the horses

If the log had to be pulled down a steep hill, it might rush down and hit the horse. To prevent this the skidder used a trick called *snubbing*. One end of the log was chained to the horse while the other end was tied to a tree at the top of the hill. As the horse pulled the log down, the rope around the tree was slowly let out.

The skidders piled their logs on skidways where the road to the river started.

46

Two horses could pull the load of 50 logs because the skidroad was icy.

The teamsters

The teamsters pulled the logs along the road to the river. After the cooks, the teamsters were first up. They had to feed and harness their horses or oxen at four in the morning. The horses were large breeds, such as Clydesdales and Percherons.

A dangerous occupation

The icy logging road could be very dangerous. On steep parts hay or sand was spread to slow the sleigh down. Sometimes the sleigh went too fast and crashed into the horses in front, breaking their legs or killing them. On one pile-up a horse had its harness ripped right off its body and was pitched into a snowbank. Luckily, it didn't even receive a scratch. Teamsters had to sit on the pile of logs to drive the horses. One time the chain for strapping the logs onto a sleigh snapped. Forty logs flew off in all directions. The teamster clung to the log he was sitting on. Luckily his log was one of the three that stayed on the sleigh.

At the end of the road by the river, the logs were piled in stacks called *rollaways*.

River drivers drove or pushed the logs down the river to the sawmill. The melting ice has made the water run quickly. The drivers push logs from the teamsters' rollaway into the river.

River drivers push stranded logs into the river. If too many logs piled up a log jam woul begin. River driving was dangerous. Crosses along the river marked river drivers' grave

When a river became completely jammed with logs, often the only way to start the logs moving again was to blast out the logs in front with dynamite.

The key log holding all the others back has begun to move. All the logs will move. Run for your life and hope your spiked shoes will carry you to safety!

River drivers lived in a tent or under a lean-to right beside the river as they followed the logs down to the sawmill. Their job was to keep the logs moving.

Each lumber camp put a timber mark on its logs. MLB stands for McLaughlin Brothers.

This girl is banging the timber mark of a star into each log with her hammer.

A huge raft of 100 cribs towed by a tug into the middle of the river to start its journey down to the sea. The men will sleep in the small huts and eat under the large roof.

The raftsmen

On larger rivers 20 pieces of squared timber were lashed together into *cribs*. Then the cribs were lashed together to make large rafts. The men lived on the rafts as they floated down the river.

The rafts would break up if they went over a waterfall. Therefore the raftsmen built a canal beside the waterfall. The canal was called a timber slide. At the top of the slide the rafts were broken down into cribs again. The cribs sped down the timber slide. At the bottom, the cribs were tied together again into a large raft. It was exciting shooting down the slide. It was like riding the log flume at an amusement park.

The raftsmen slept on the rafts in little wooden huts. They cooked their meals on board. The firewood was burned on a bed of sand so the wooden timbers of the raft would not catch fire. It was a cambuse fireplace just like the fireplace in the shanty they had just left. And the food was the same as in the shanty. Lots of beans! Beans for breakfast, lunch and supper. They amused themselves by

singing and dancing as they floated down the river.

Sometimes the raftsmen could not stop the large raft before it went over the falls. Then the raft would break up. The raftsmen would be thrown into the rushing waters. Many would drown. The wooden crosses over their graves could be seen on the bank of the river beside all the falls and rapids.

The raftsmen steered with long oars called sweeps. The logs of the raft were held together by wooden pegs. The raftsmen used the pegs as oar locks as they steered the raft through the many rapids.

Though life was dangerous on the rafts, the raftsmen knew that when they brought their raft safely down the river to the city, they would be paid. Then they could enjoy meeting their friends who had sailed down the river on other rafts. They would have a party with old friends. And they could go home to their farms until next autumn, when the lumber camp would be set up again. Then the chopping, skidding and, later, the river driving would begin all over again.

51

The large raft would have been smashed to pieces sailing over the falls. The river drivers broke the large raft into cribs again. The cribs are floated down a timber

slide. The slide was especially made as a method of getting around the falls. It was easier to float the cribs down the slide than to carry them over a portage.

A raftsman dances a fast, happy jig. There was usually someone on a raft who could play the fiddle. The raftsmen sang the songs of their different countries.

Raftsmen eat lunch. The logs for the cooking fire were burned on top of sand so that the raft wouldn't catch fire. You can see smoke rising from the fire under the roof.

Rising and falling, a raft plunges down the rapids. One raftsman holds on to a mast so he won't be thrown overboard. Often the raft broke up on the rocks.

In this old photograph raftsmen dash about to help their raft through the rapids. You can see how the raft is bending as it roars down the dangerous rapids.

A huge raft has arrived at the seaport. The squared timber will be loaded onto the sailing ships in the background. The timber will be sold in England and Europe.

Wood for the world

The forests of England and Europe were growing smaller. They could not produce all the wood that England and the countries of Europe needed. They needed wood from the forests of North America. The square timber from the river rafts was shipped over the Atlantic Ocean. Because the timber was square it fit easily into the hold of the sailing ship. Some of the wood was used to build ships. The tallest and straightest trees were used to make masts for the ships' sails.

Now that the raftsmen had safely brought their rafts to the sailing port, they were able to enjoy themselves. Some of them drank too much alcohol. When they passed out they were often carried aboard the timber ships. They were forced to become sailors. They sailed to Europe with the same logs that they rafted down the river

Men break up cribs and load the square timber into a sailing ship's hold.

A logger in his red sash does a lively jig beside the cambuse fire. Sunday was the one day the loggers didn't work. Singing and dancing were two of their favorite pastimes.

Sunday, one day to play

Loggers worked very hard. But they found time for entertainment. Every Saturday night someone would be fiddling on a violin. Men would dance the jigs and reels of their native lands: Quebec, Ireland, England, Scotland, Norway, Sweden, Finland. They leapt about in dances from Poland and the Ukraine.

There were usually no women at the lumber camps, so some of the loggers would tie flour sacks around their waists as skirts and handkerchiefs around their arms as frilly sleeves. These bearded loggers were the women in the dances.

Stories of past heroes

Games such as Blindman's Bluff were fun. And so were the storytellers. They told ghost stories about headless men prowling the woods that made their friends' blood run cold with fear. And they told stories about the bravery of loggers they had known and the great trees they had cut down.

Loggers liked all kinds of card games. Here a game attracts a big audience.

Giant cedars dwarf two loggers. The roots made a large swelling at the base of the tree. The tree was too thick for loggers to cut it down while standing on the ground.

Western logging

The west coast of North America was a lumberman's paradise. The trees were huge. The Douglas firs and the redwoods towered seventy metres in the air. The early settlers could drive a stagecoach through a hollowed-out cut trunk. You could even drive a stagecoach along the trunk of these fallen giants.

The great trees of the west coast were hard to cut down. There were huge bulges at the base of the trees where the roots spread out into the soil. The tree was too thick to cut through if you stood on the ground to chop it. The loggers cut holes in the trees six feet off the ground and stuck planks into them. They stood on the planks to cut the tree down, one on one side of the front cut and one on the other. When the tree began to fall the men jumped from their perch and ran like mad to escape falling branches. These branches were called *widow-makers*.

In the rain forests of the west coast the climate was too mild to have ice roads. The teamsters had to build corduroy skid-roads. These were logs laid side by side through the forest. The logs of the skid road were greased with whale oil, bear grease or even butter to make it easier for the oxen to pull the huge trees over them. Later, around 1900, the lumbermen began to use donkeys to pull the huge trees out of the forest. Donkeys were steam engines. Steel wires from the donkeys were attached to the trees. The donkey's engine pulled in the wire, hauling the tree out of the forest. This was easier than skidding with oxen.

A new axe was developed for the trees of the west coast. A double-bladed axe with a long handle cut more deeply into giant trees, such as the Douglas fir.

Loggers use the long-handled double-headed western axe. They stand on springboards to make the front cut.

After 1880 saws made the back cut. The tree will fall toward the front cut.

The west coast trees were so large that loggers often had to split them in two with dynamite. They cut off the bark so they would slide more easily over the skidroad.

Loggers set up a skidroad. They will fill the spaces between the logs with dirt, leaving the tops of the logs showing. The trees will slide across the round logs.

A team of 14 oxen pulls a turn of four logs down a skidroad. The bull puncher stands ready with his stick to prod his team forward.

The loggers attached the wire to the huge log. The donkey engine wound the wire around the spool, pulling the log out of the forest. Loggers rode on the logs for fun.

On the west coast, train engines were used to pull the logs from the end of the skidroad to the sawmill.

Loggers dress up on Sunday, their one day off. Their families have come to visit. It's a lovely autumn day. In a few weeks snow will be on the ground.

The logger's family at camp

A foreman stands in front of his cabin with his wife and child.

Because most of the early loggers were farmers, their wives and children could not come with them to the logging camp. The wives and children had more important jobs to do at home. They had to keep the farm running properly. They had to feed and care for the livestock; the cows, pigs, sheep and chickens.

The early logging camp usually had one shanty in which all the men slept, including the foreman, the teamsters and the cook. There was no room for families.

When the logging camps became larger sometimes a few separate buildings were put up so that the foreman and perhaps the cook could bring their families.

The wives did useful jobs. They taught the cook how to make food that tasted better. They often ran a laundry service, charging the men money for washing their shirts and socks. The life in the logging camp improved when families came.

Glossary

adze *a tool designed to scoop wood out of a log*

auger *a tool for drilling holes in wood*

bee *settlers work together to do one neighbor's work*

broadax *a special axe for squaring logs*

blacksmith *made and put shoes on horses; also made iron tools*

bull of the woods *the foreman of the logging camp*

bull puncher *logger who skids logs out of the forest using oxen*

bush *forest*

cabinetmaker *a person who makes furniture*

cambuse fire *an open fireplace with the logs placed on a bed of sand*

chopper *a logger who cuts trees down*

contract chopper *person who cleared settlers' land for money*

cooper *a person who makes barrels*

crib *20 logs lashed together to form a small raft*

cruiser *a person who searched the forest for the best trees to cut*

donkey *a steam engine that skidded logs out of the forest*

finishing mill *a sawmill that produced smooth wood for craftsmen. It also often made doors, stairway railings and wall moldings*

gunsmith *a person who makes and repairs guns*

hewer *a logger who squared timber*

lean-to *a shelter made of branches*

logging bee *settlers cut down trees to clear a neighbor's land*

milldam *a dam built to hold back water to make a millpond*

millpond *the widened river behind the milldam*

millrace *the channel through which water flows from the millpond to the waterwheel*

muley saw *the earliest sawmill saw that cut wood by moving up and down*

planing mill *a sawmill that produced smooth wood for craftsmen*

raftsmen *loggers who sailed a raft of logs down the river*

river driver *a logger who keeps logs moving down the river to the sawmill*

rollaway *a pile of logs by the river waiting for the spring ice breakup*

rotary saw *a round saw that cut wood by moving in a circle*

sawyer *a person who cuts wood in a sawmill. He was not necessarily the sawmill owner.*

shanty *the log building in which loggers slept and ate*

skid *to haul logs out of the forest*

skidder *the logger who hauls logs out of the forest to the skidway*

skidroad *logs half-buried in earth over which trees are skidded out of the forest*

skidway *a pile of logs at the start of the road to the river*

springboard *a plank on which western loggers stood to cut down trees*

teamster *a logger who hauls logs from the skidway to the river*

wainwright *a person who makes and repairs wagons and carriages*

waterwheel *a wheel turned by water that made the saw operate*

whipsaw *a two-person saw for cutting planks from a log*

Index

Acknowledgements

Library of Congress, Colonial Williamsburg, Harper's Weekly, The American Agriculturalist, Scugog Shores Historical Museum, Port Perry, Department of Industry and Tourism, Illustrated Magazine of Art, Ontario Archives, Metropolitan Toronto Library, Upper Canada Village, Public Archives of Canada, Century Village, Lang, The Hope Sawmill, Marc Crabtree, Peter Crabtree, Bobbie Kalman.

1415 LB Printed in the U.S.A. 98